BRODY'S GHOST

BOOK 1

STORY AND ART BY
MARK CRILLEY

DARK HORSE BOOKS

THIS BOOK IS DEDICATED TO JILL THOMPSON,
WHO BELIEVED IN THIS SERIES
WHEN I'D ALMOST STOPPED
BELIEVING IN IT MYSELF.

Publisher – Mike Richardson
Designer – Justin Couch
Assistant Editor – Patrick Thorpe
Associate Editor – Katie Moody
Editor – Dave Land
Assistant Collection Editor – Jemiah Jefferson
Collection Editor – Rachel Edidin

Published by Dark Horse Books
A division of Dark Horse Comics, Inc.
10956 SE Main Street
Milwaukie, OR 97222

DarkHorse.com

To find a comic shop in your area call the
Comic Shop Locator Service toll-free at (888) 266-4226

Scholastic edition: July 2011
ISBN 978-1-59582-834-7

This book collects Brody's Ghost Volumes 1 and 2.

1 3 5 7 9 10 8 6 4 2
Printed at Transcontinental Gagné, Louiseville, QC, Canada

SHUP
SHUP SHUP

TIPS

KREEEEEEEEE

Weird.

The truck had been there all afternoon.

But not the girl.

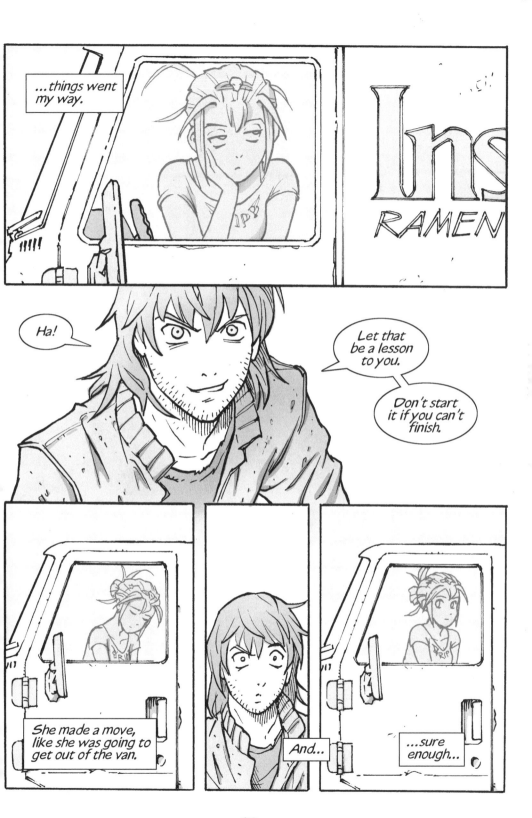

Gramma, lookit that man over there.

What's wrong with him?

Hush, darling. It's not polite to stare at...

...

BAIL BONDS

...troubled people.

You're not listening to me, are you?

Huh? Oh.

Sorry, Gabe. I had a really...

...weird day today.

Oh yeah? What happened?

I...

...saw...

...

What? What'd ya see?

I saw this guy.

This guy who knows Nicole.

36

47

50

Talia led me across town to a condemned stretch of overpass the city had never gotten around to tearing down.

Withered flowers marked the exact spot where the Penny Murderer had taken his most recent victim...

...a 22-year-old law student by the name of Ashley Lindstrom.

Talia disappeared for a couple of weeks.

One night, after saving up a pretty good stash of dough, I put on my best clothes and went to Arturo's...

...the swanky restaurant where my ex-girlfriend Nicole worked as a waitress.

I knew trying to patch things back up with her was the longest of long shots...

...but I had to give it a try. One last time.

Brody, what are you doing here?

I told you never to come to this place.

Five minutes, Nicole.

That's all I'm asking for.

I'll spare you the painful details.

Hey, Longhair...

...didn't nobody tell you this is a toll road?

You owe us money.

Members of the L47s. They'd been running the streets in that part of town for years.

I'd had my little run-ins with them in the past. Something told me tonight was going to be different.

I don't owe you anything.

I love it when they try to talk tough.

Heh heh

You're gonna pay the toll.

And tonight the toll is...

...everything you got on you.

Now, that bit of lip you just gave me means you're gettin' beat up either way.

But if you get down on your knees and hand the money over right now...

...along with a very...

...very sincere apology...

...you'll still be able to walk when we're done with you.

68

73

Talia led me from what was already one of the city's shabbier neighborhoods to a part of town people called the Off Grid.

It was kind of a black hole of public services: No police, no firefighters, no garbage collection.

There, on the other side of a barbed-wire fence and a graveyard of rusting refrigerators, we reached our final destination...

...Shinshoji Temple.

It had been built by a community of Japanese immigrants...

...one that had evidently moved somewhere more worthy of human habitation.

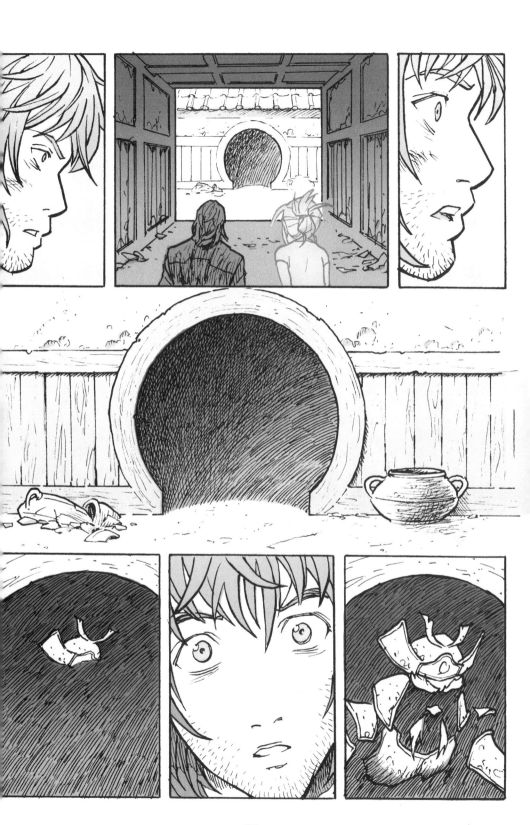

...and cause it to levitate.

Levitate?!

Close-range object levitation.

The standard litmus test for any ghostseer.

Sensei, with all due respect...

...I think maybe you and I need to have a little chat.

You know...

...ghost to ghost.

After intense negotiations, Talia managed to alter the test to something she considered much more "in my league."

The book was soon turned upright, its spine cracked just enough to keep it balanced in that position.

The task now...

...which Talia assured me was very doable...

...was to knock it over with the power of my mind.

But Talia--

You can do this. I know you can.

And Brody...

85

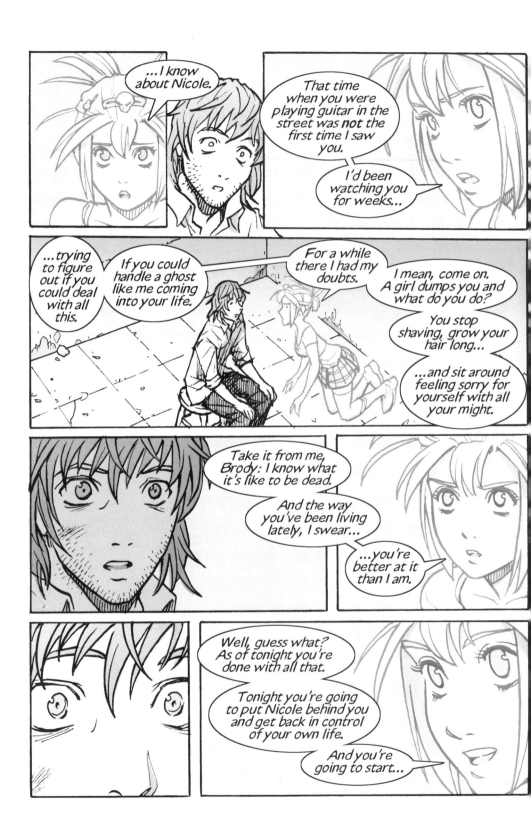

...by passing this one simple test.

You're ready, Brody.

Now go ahead and do it.

The room went silent as I focused my mind on the book and tried to do as I was told.

A minute went by.

Then five, then ten.

The book stayed absolutely where it was. Not the slightest sign of **anything**.

Somewhere around fifteen minutes, Kagemura broke the silence.

He is not what you believe him to be, child.

He is just another ghostseer.

Wait! Give him more time.

He's almost there...

It's over, Talia.

87

88

PART 2

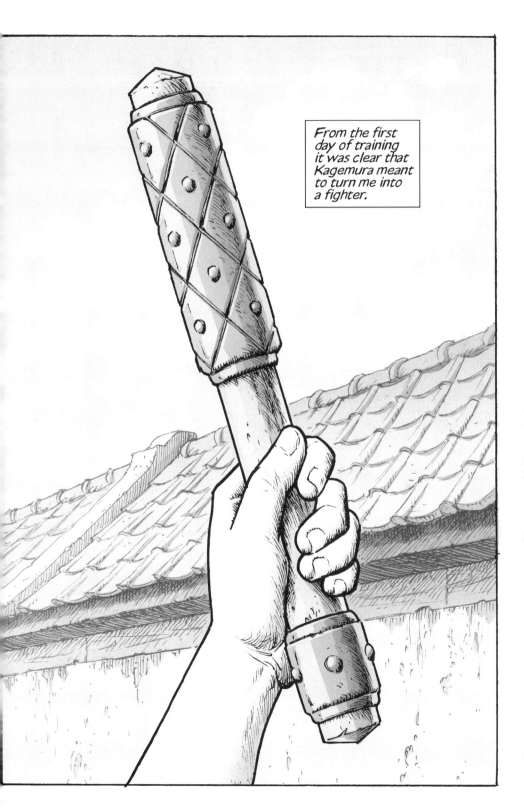

From the first day of training it was clear that Kagemura meant to turn me into a fighter.

He presented me with a wood-and-steel club he called the "kanazuchi."

In the right hands, he said, it could knock any opponent unconscious with a single blow to the head.

The first weeks were devoted to exercise.

Long painful hours of it, from sunrise to sunset.

It was brutal. I'd gone my whole life without working out. Now I was suddenly doing little else.

Kagemura had this thing about making me climb utility poles.

One day he challenged me to climb a hundred of them by nightfall.

I did it.

The next morning my arms were on fire.

I soon reached the point where I could scale even the highest in under a minute.

In the third week of training Kagemura formally introduced me to his demighosts.

Every morning he had me face off against one of them.

They were each masters of a different combat style.

For the one called Soku...

...it was speed.

For Chi, it was all about strategy and intellect.

They were long, hard, painful lessons.

But that was only half of the training.

The rest was devoted to developing my psychic powers.

Strange stuff: Almost like torture.

Solitary confinement.

Shouting at walls.

Hanging upside down for hours on end.

One exercise consisted of lying flat on my back and having Chi tap me lightly on the forehead with a bamboo stick.

Ten thousand times.

The breakthrough, when it finally came, was small.

An extinguished candle.
A trail of smoke.

But I will say this.

Any attempt to make use of your powers outside of my training methods will end in failure.

If I find that you have been making such attempts...

...I will halt the training at once.

Is that understood?

Yes, Master.

The following morning Kagemura took the unusual step of leaving Shinshoji Temple and coming to inspect my apartment.

Brody, would it kill you to at least throw out the rotting food every once in a while?

You've got half a pizza over there with mold on it an inch high.

There's half a pizza in here?

It didn't take long to separate out the items Kagemura deemed essential.

Clothes. A blanket. Eating utensils. A toothbrush. And a book of matches.

I wanted to keep my pillow but he said rolled-up clothing would suffice.

Everything else I was told to pile up on the other side of the room.

Before I brought you to Kagemura your idea of a good time was sitting on the street...

...living off pity money from people who wished you could play something else besides "Stairway to Heaven."

Yeah, well that was *my* life, Talia.

I *chose* it.

No one chose it *for* me.

You may have chosen it...

...but that doesn't make it a *life*.

You can kid yourself that this is all about you "standing up for who you are"...

...but I'm not buying it.

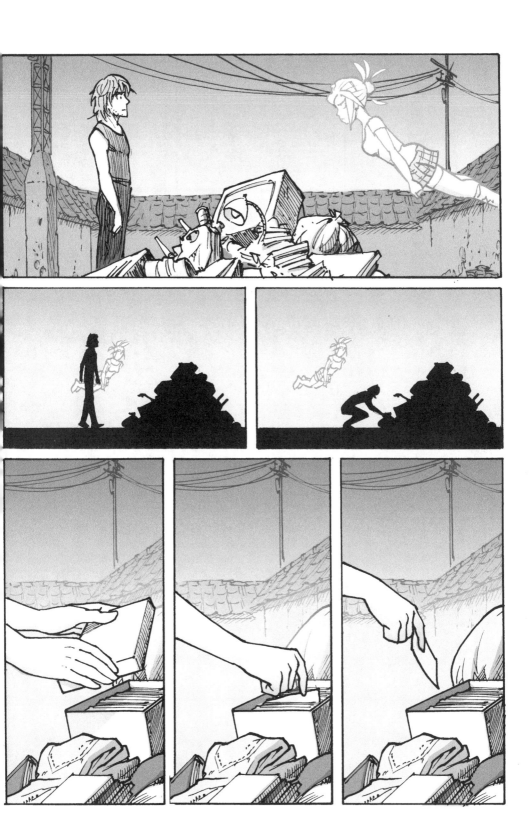

FFFFTCH

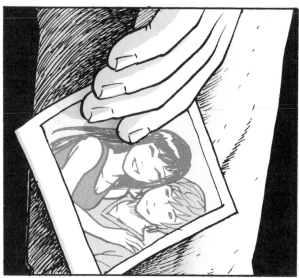

When I woke up the next morning...

...it took me a while to figure out whose apartment I was in.

Kagemura was right, of course: Destroying my possessions freed me from the past and vastly improved my progress in the training.

I began to absorb the various fighting skills of each of the demighosts...

...and, in time...

...learned to identify and exploit their various hidden weaknesses.

My supernatural abilities improved as well.

Kagemura taught me how to make objects levitate.

I could soon raise lightweight objects into the air--

--paper, bits of string--

--and cause them to move as I wished.

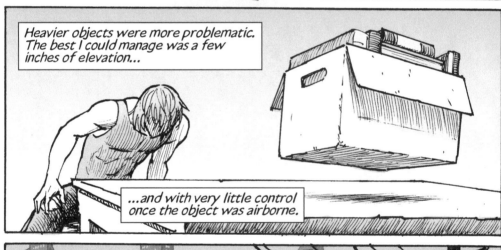

Heavier objects were more problematic. The best I could manage was a few inches of elevation...

...and with very little control once the object was airborne.

One night Kagemura said I was ready to enter the final phase of the training.

You know you're in for something pretty intense when the first thing they do is tie you down.

Master...

...can I at least know what's about to happen to me?

This is the hour of your transformation, Living One.

Tonight you become what you were always meant to be.

And, uh...

...just what exactly is that?

You will know soon enough.

GYAAAAAAAAAAAAAAGH!!!

The next day, when I undid the bandages, I saw what they'd done to me.

I saw it.

That doesn't mean I understood it.

The L47s had set up shop on the top floor of a condemned office building.

...the old man had been prepping me for this from day one.

155

Drop it, man.

Just drop it...

...before I put a bullet in your face.

160

...how many of his boys do I have to pop before he...

Hold on.

I know you.

You ain't with Marcello.

You're that dude Mikey beat up.

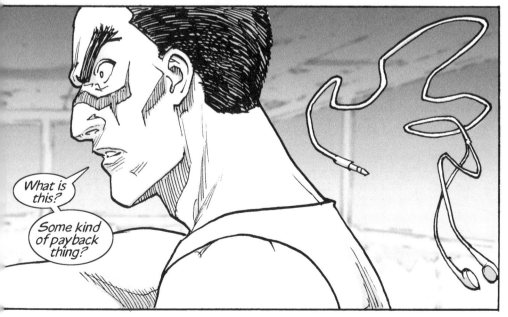

What is this?

Some kind of payback thing?

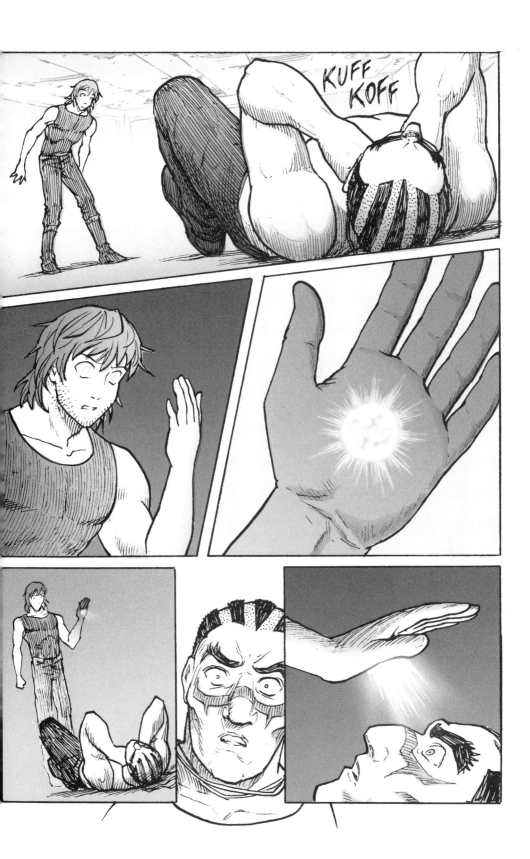

I couldn't afford a doctor, so I went back to Shinshoji Temple.

There one of the demighosts treated my wound...

...while Kagemura debriefed me about what had happened at the end of my fight with the L47s.

The purification rite you performed upon him is an ancient one.

It comes by instinct to all who have completed the training.

What did it do to him?

You have broken his spirit, Living One.

When he awakens he will find himself in a greatly weakened state.

His vision dimmed...

...his mind clouded...

...his body prematurely aged and feeble.

In time he will be cast aside by the criminal world...

...and the group he led will dissolve into squabbling factions.

Wait a minute. You said, "successfully completed the training."

You mean I'm done?

There are many higher levels to which you may ascend if you so choose.

But yes...

...you have learned the essentials of what I wish to teach you for now.

Kagemura told me to spend the following weeks in contemplation. When I felt the time was right...

...I was to come to him with a decision about whether I wished to ascend to the "higher levels" of the training.

A lot happened during those days.

For starters, I finally gave in and got that haircut Talia had been pestering me about.

Yeah.

That's great.

I even shaved.

Ow.

Cut myself to ribbons, too.

It had been a while.

174

And that was it.

She walked off without another word...

...turning to flash me one last smile...

...as she strolled away down the sidewalk.

And me, I just stood there...

...shaking from head to toe...

...trying to convince myself that what I'd just seen wasn't real.

But I knew that all I could say for sure...

...was that it wasn't real yet.

HOW TO DRAW TALIA

The trick to drawing Talia—or any character, really—is getting all the lines in the right spot. For the beginning artist it's best to start with a few penciled guidelines.

1. Start with a circle.

2. Add the lines as shown. Note that line A cuts the circle in half; line B divides it into quarters. Note also the distance between the circle and the point of the chin: slightly greater than the distance between lines A and B.

(A)

(B)

3. Add the eyes first, noting how they touch both line B and the edge of the circle. The nostrils fall just below the circle; the mouth is about halfway between the circle and the tip of the chin. Note the angles when placing the lines of the hair.

4. Add the eyebrows, noting the angles and the fact they are slightly closer to the eyes than to line A. Add the irises to the eyes, paying special attention to where they rest within each eye. People will notice if the placement of the facial features is off; with the hair it's all a bit more random, so feel free to experiment with that part of the drawing. (I draw those strands of hair slightly differently every time, to be honest!)

5. Add the details: lines above each eye to indicate eyelids and eyelashes, a line below the mouth for the lip, lines dividing the hair into smaller strands, and of course the all-important barrettes in the hair.

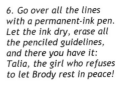

6. Go over all the lines with a permanent-ink pen. Let the ink dry, erase all the penciled guidelines, and there you have it: Talia, the girl who refuses to let Brody rest in peace!

Looking for something new to read?

CHECK OUT THESE OTHER GREAT TITLES FROM DARK HORSE BOOKS!

Join Usagi Yojimbo in his hare-raising adventures of life and death. Watch as he faces assassins, medicine peddlers, bat ninjas, and more, in this twenty-volumes-and-counting epic! This is a story of honor and adventure, a masterful adaptation of samurai legend to sequential art. Dark Horse is proud to present this Eisner award-winning and internationally acclaimed tour de force by master storyteller Stan Sakai!

Lulu Moppet is the true-blue daughter of Main Street America, clever and sweet, mischievous and generous, an eight-year-old hero for anyone who ever wanted to bring home a gorilla, scare the pants off of ghosts, and outwit every grownup in sight. With eleven volumes already available (and many more, including a color special, on the way!), there are plenty of chances to discover why generations of readers have considered *Little Lulu* one of smartest, cutest, and funniest comics ever to hit the shelves!

Just how much trouble can a toy animal really cause? Find out in this funny, unsettling, and utterly endearing series written and drawn by Tony Millionaire! Follow along with mischievous sock monkey Uncle Gabby and bumbling bird Drinky Crow as they try to find a home for a shrunken head, try their hands at matchmaking, hunt salamanders and butterflies, tackle home repairs, face off against creatures from the deep, and try to get to heaven. Delights! Happy endings and random destruction are guaranteed! Check out any of the amazing *Sock Monkey* stories already out and about, or hop on board for the latest *Sock Monkey* yarn, *The Inches Incident*.

Find out more about these and other great Dark Horse all-ages titles at darkhorse.com!

AVAILABLE AT YOUR LOCAL COMICS SHOP OR BOOKSTORE
TO FIND A COMICS SHOP IN YOUR AREA, CALL 1-888-266-4226

For more information or to order direct: •On the web: darkhorse.com •E-mail: mailorder@darkhorse.com •Phone: 1-800-862-0052
Mon.-Fri. 9 A.M. to 5 P.M. Pacific Time.
Usagi Yojimbo © 2006 by Stan Sakai. Little Lulu © 2006 by Classic Media, Inc. Sock Monkey © 2006 by Tony Millionaire. (BL 6000)